Chocolate

GENERAL EDITOR
CHUCK WILLIAMS

RECIPES
LORA BRODY

PHOTOGRAPHY
ALLAN ROSENBERG

TIME
LIFE
BOOKS

Time-Life Books
is a division of TIME LIFE INC.,
a wholly owned subsidiary of
THE TIME INC. BOOK COMPANY

President: John M. Fahey

TIME-LIFE BOOKS
President: John Hall
Vice President and Publisher, Custom Publishing:
    Susan J. Maruyama
Director of Custom Publishing: Frances C. Mangan
Director of Marketing: Nancy K. Jones

WILLIAMS-SONOMA
Founder/Vice-Chairman: Chuck Williams

WELDON OWEN INC.
President: John Owen
Publisher: Wendely Harvey
Managing Editor: Laurie Wertz
Consulting Editor: Norman Kolpas
Copy Editor: Sharon Silva
Editorial Assistant: Janique Poncelet
Design: John Bull, The Book Design Company
Production: Stephanie Sherman, Mick Bagnato
Food Photographer: Allan Rosenberg
Associate Food Photographer: Allen V. Lott
Primary Food & Prop Stylist: Sandra Griswold
Food Stylist: Heidi Gintner
Assistant Food Stylist: Danielle Di Salvo
Prop Assistant: Karen Nicks
Glossary Illustrations: Alice Harth

The Williams-Sonoma Kitchen Library
conceived and produced by Weldon Owen Inc.
814 Montgomery St., San Francisco, CA 94133

In collaboration with Williams-Sonoma
100 North Point, San Francisco, CA 94133

Production by Mandarin Offset, Hong Kong
Printed in China

A Note on Weights and Measures:
All recipes include customary U.S., U.K. and
metric measurements. Conversions are based on
a standard developed for these books and have
been rounded off. Actual weights may vary.

A Weldon Owen Production

Library of Congress
Cataloging-in-Publication Data:

Brody, Lora, 1945-
    Chocolate / general editor, Chuck Williams ;
recipes, Lora Brody ; photography,
Allan Rosenberg.
        p.   cm. — (Williams-Sonoma
    kitchen library)
    Includes index.
    ISBN 0-7835-0241-9 (trade) ;
    ISBN 0-7835-0242-7 (library)
    1. Cookery (Chocolate) 2. Desserts.
    I. Williams, Chuck. II. Title.   III. Series.
TX767.C5B75 1993
641.6'374—dc20   93-17990
                                       CIP

Contents

CANDIES 17

FROZEN DESSERTS 31

PUDDINGS 45

CAKES, PIES & COOKIES 55

INTRODUCTION

The 18th-century Swedish botanist Carl von Linnaeus wisely named the tropical tree from which we get chocolate *Theobroma*, a compound of Greek words meaning "food of the gods." Every chocolate lover—myself included—would readily agree with his decision: Nothing compares with the rich, sweet flavor or luscious melting texture of chocolate, and any recipe in which it stars appears to be heaven-sent.

This book is a celebration of chocolate. It begins with a few introductory lessons: tips on buying the ingredient in all its many forms, how to chop and melt it with ease, and the secrets to making elaborate-looking yet surprisingly simple decorative effects.

Following these basics are four chapters that run the gamut of chocolate creativity, with 44 recipes for chocolate candies, fudges, truffles and dipped fruits; ice creams and other frozen desserts; and cakes, puddings, cookies and pies.

These easy-to-follow recipes, each of which is accompanied by a full-page color photograph, will make chocolate cookery more tempting and satisfying than ever before. And a comprehensive glossary of ingredients and techniques will help to ensure success with every recipe. Dessert making takes patience, especially working with chocolate. Before starting a recipe, read it through completely so that you understand it and have all of the ingredients.

Let me add one important piece of advice here: Always start with the best-quality chocolate you can find in specialty-food stores and good food markets. Finer in texture, richer and more flavorful, the best chocolate is also easier to work with, which produces more reliable results. The relatively small extra expense for outstanding imported or domestic products will be far exceeded by the pleasure you and your guests will receive from baked goods, candies and desserts that look and taste like a gift from heaven.

EQUIPMENT

Special equipment for baking and candy making will help you create chocolate desserts at their best

Making desserts and confections with chocolate calls for a few pieces of specialized equipment to ensure the featured ingredient is shown off at its finest. A double boiler and an instant-read thermometer, for example, both safeguard chocolate during melting.

Baking calls for greater precision than most other forms of cooking. Good measuring tools will help you achieve the necessary accuracy. Pans and tins of the sizes and shapes specified in the recipes in this book will produce the most reliable results.

1. Baking Pans and Sheets
A wide variety of shapes and sizes for baking cakes, cookies and quick breads, and for holding fudges and other candies. Choose good-quality heavy aluminum or tinplate steel, which conducts heat well for fast, even baking.

2. Metal Pie Pan
Metal—preferably aluminum—conducts heat best for a crisp, browned crust. Standard size is 9 inches (23 cm), measured inside the rim. If using black steel or dark anodized aluminum, which absorbs heat faster, the oven temperature may need to be reduced by 25°F (15°C).

3. Muffin Tins
Tins for baking miniature (about 1½ tablespoons) and standard (about 3½ fl oz/110 ml) cupcakes. Small cupcakes may take a few minutes less to bake than standard ones. Whenever possible, choose nonstick tins. If they have dark surfaces, which absorb heat more easily, oven temperature may need to be reduced by 25°F (15°C) or baking time may need to be shortened.

4. Double Boiler
A set of two stacked pans: a lower pan for holding simmering water and a smaller top pan for gently heating chocolate or other heat-sensitive food.

5. Piping Bag and Tips
Plastic-lined cloth or all-plastic bag and stainless-steel tips enable easy, accurate piping of whipped cream or other decorative toppings.

6. Steamed Pudding Mold
Stainless-steel mold with watertight lid, for containing puddings that cook in a steamer.

7. Instant-Read Thermometer
Provides a quick, accurate reading of temperature—essential for gauging water temperature when melting chocolate for dipping (see recipe on page 18).

8. Liquid Measuring Cup
For accurate measuring of liquid ingredients. Choose heavy-duty heat-resistant glass, marked on one side in cups and ounces, on the other in milliliters. Lip and handle facilitate pouring.

9. Dry Measuring Cups
In graduated sizes, for precise measuring of dry ingredients. Straight rims allow ingredients to be leveled for accuracy. Choose stainless steel for precision and sturdiness.

10. Measuring Spoons
In graduated sizes, for measuring small quantities of ingredients such as baking powder and salt. Select good-quality, calibrated metal spoons with deep bowls.

11. Round Cake Pan
Traditional circular pan for layer and other kinds of cakes. Usually comes in 8- and 9-inch (20- and 23-cm) sizes. Choose good-quality, seamless, heavy metal pans. Available with removable base.

12. Springform Pans
Circular and tube pans with spring-clip sides that loosen for easy unmolding of delicate cakes that might stick.

13. Parchment Paper
For lining cake pans or baking sheets to prevent sticking. Waxed paper can also be used.

14. Wire Whisks
For beating eggs or blending liquids before incorporating them into batters. Choose stainless steel. Use the shorter balloon whisk for whisking egg whites.

15. Glass Pie Dish
Attractive container for baking and serving pie. Holds heat well for crisp, brown crusts. Choose good-quality ovenproof glass.

16. Wire Cooling Racks
Allows air to circulate under baked cakes, pies and cookies for quick, even cooling. Varied shapes and sizes suit different kinds of bakeware.

17. Oven Thermometer
Good-quality thermometer that can hang from or stand on an oven rack. Used to calibrate an oven's temperature for more accurate baking.

18. Rolling Pin with Handles
The most commonly used rolling pin for pie dough. Choose one with ball-bearing handles for smooth rolling, and a hardwood surface at least 12 inches (30 cm) long. Wider diameter is better for pastry making. To prevent warping, do not wash; wipe clean with a dry cloth.

19. Sifter
For sifting together dry ingredients or for sifting flour before measuring, in cake recipes that call for sifted flour. May also be used to sift confectioners' (icing) sugar to decorate desserts.

20. Long Metal Spatula
For spreading frosting or cutting brownies and bar cookies.

21. Zester
Small, sharp holes at end of stainless-steel blade cut citrus zest into fine shreds. Choose a model with a sturdy, well-attached handle.

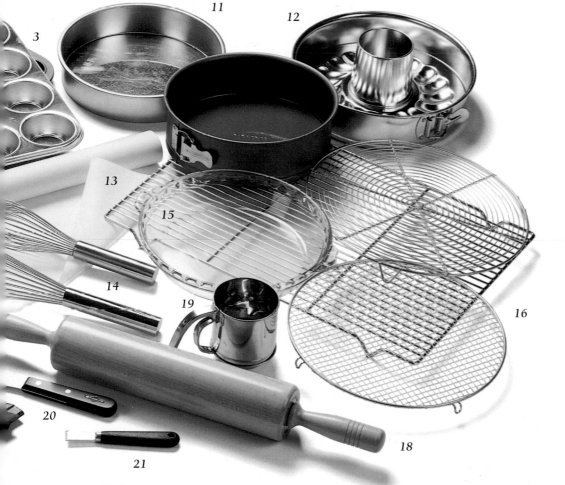

CHOCOLATE BASICS

From the seeds of the tropical cacao tree comes a bounty of chocolate products

Chocolate is made from the seeds, or beans, of the tropical cacao tree. Fermented to develop their flavor and to loosen the pulp that surrounds them, cacao beans, also known as cocoa beans, are then dried, cleaned, sorted, roasted and cracked. The resulting small nibs of cacao are ground under high pressure to form chocolate liquor, a dark brown, fine paste whose fluidity reflects the fact that about 54 percent of its total weight consists of the fat known as cocoa butter.

This liquor, solidified in blocks, becomes the most basic product for the kitchen: bitter, unsweetened chocolate. Further refined through repeated milling (called conching), and mixed with varying proportions of sugar and additional cocoa butter, the chocolate grows smoother and gradually lighter in color, becoming bittersweet, semisweet and sweet chocolate. Because the depth of the chocolate flavor and the degree of sweetness of each chocolate type vary with the manufacturer, bittersweet, semisweet and sweet chocolates are generally interchangeable in recipes, depending upon individual tastes. The addition of milk solids to sweetened chocolate creates creamy milk chocolate.

Cocoa butter alone, filtered free of the chocolate liquor's dark solids under hydraulic pressure and then enhanced with milk, sugar and sometimes vanilla, produces so-called white chocolate. And the chocolate solids minus the cocoa butter, ground to a fine powder, become the various forms of cocoa.

Whatever kind of chocolate or cocoa you buy, store it in a cool, dry place at temperatures ranging from 55°–65°F (12°–18°C). Do not freeze or refrigerate. To prevent chocolate from absorbing the aromas of other foods, keep it tightly wrapped. Store cocoa powder in an airtight container to safeguard against humidity.

1. Unsweetened chocolate
Pure chocolate liquor ground from roasted cacao beans and solidified in block-shaped molds. Unpalatable when eaten on its own. Combined with sugar and butter, milk or cream in recipes, it provides intense chocolate flavor. Also known as bitter chocolate.

2. Sweet chocolate
Form of eating or cooking chocolate to which sugar and cocoa butter have been added. Generally sweeter than semi-sweet and bittersweet chocolate.

3. Bittersweet chocolate
Eating or cooking chocolate enriched with cocoa butter and sweetened with sugar, which accounts for approximately 40 percent of its weight, although the percentage may vary.

4. Semisweet chocolate
Eating or cooking chocolate that is usually—but not always—slightly sweeter than bittersweet chocolate. Bittersweet chocolate may be substituted.

5

7

6

9

8

First, break the chocolate by hand into small chunks, handling it as little as possible to avoid melting. Then, using a heavy knife and a clean, dry, odor-free chopping surface, carefully chop it into smaller pieces.

Steadying the knife tip with your hand, continue chopping across the pieces until the desired consistency is reached.

5. Semisweet chocolate chips
Semisweet chocolate that has been molded into small drop shapes, for uniform incorporation into batters.

6. Milk chocolate
Primarily an eating chocolate, enriched with powdered milk—the equivalent of up to 1 cup (8 fl oz/250 ml) whole milk in the average-sized candy bar.

7. Unsweetened cocoa
Fine-textured powder ground from the solids left after much of the cocoa butter has been extracted from chocolate liquor. Richly flavored, it is also naturally acidic, reacting with baking soda (bicarbonate of soda) to create carbon dioxide gas that leavens baked goods.

8. White Chocolate
A chocolatelike product for eating or cooking, made by combining pure cocoa butter with sugar, powdered milk and sometimes vanilla. Check labels to make sure that the white chocolate you buy is made exclusively with cocoa butter, without the addition of coconut oil or vegetable shortening.

9. Dutch-processed cocoa
Cocoa powder specially treated to reduce its acidity, resulting in a darker color and more mellow flavor. Burns more easily than non-Dutch-processed cocoa; use the latter when high temperatures are required.

TO MELT CHOCOLATE

Chocolate scorches easily, especially when direct heat is applied; and heat that is too high will ruin it. Gentle, indirect heat is therefore necessary when melting chocolate.

Candy making calls for even greater care to keep cocoa butter from rising to the surface and forming a harmless powdery white "bloom." A process known as "tempering" (see recipe, page 18) keeps the chocolate stable and attractive.

Melting in a double boiler. Partially fill the bottom of a double boiler with water and bring to a low simmer. Put chocolate and any other ingredients to be melted in the top pan and stir gently over the heat until the chocolate is fluid. Take care that the pan doesn't touch the water or that the water does not create steam.

Making your own double boiler. Set a heatproof bowl on the rim of a large saucepan that is smaller than the bowl. Fill the saucepan with enough water to come close to the bottom of the bowl without touching it. Bring the water to a low simmer, add the chocolate to the bowl and stir gently until melted.

Melting in a microwave oven. Put chocolate pieces in a microwaveproof glass bowl and place in the microwave set on high for 20 seconds. Remove the bowl and stir. Repeat as needed until the chocolate is not quite thoroughly melted, then stir so the chocolate's own heat completes the melting process.

DECORATING WITH CHOCOLATE

Easy ways to embellish chocolate desserts, from fancy whipped cream rosettes to simple shavings

Chocolate desserts and candies are made even more special when crowned with chocolate decorations or other complementary ingredients. These beautiful flourishes are all surprisingly simple work.

Chocolate shavings and curls are among the easiest embellishments of all. By varying the tool you use and the size and temperature of the chocolate block, you can produce anything from fine particles for scattering over a pudding or ice cream to elegant curls for topping a cake or pastry. Shavings and curls can be made ahead of time and stored in an airtight container in a cool, dry place; do not refrigerate.

Piping from a pastry bag with a decorative tip or through the snipped corner of a self-sealing heavy-duty plastic bag creates a range of decorations, from whipped cream rosettes to fine chocolate writing. And stenciling with confectioners' (icing) sugar or cocoa adds yet another attractive dimension. Although piping and stenciling require some coordination, the novice can practice first on waxed paper.

Chocolate drizzles
For an abstract design as shown here on chocolate mint squares (page 76), melt the chocolate and then use a large spoon to drizzle it freehand back and forth across the dessert.

Chocolate writing
Melt chocolate or ganache (page 12) and spoon into a heavy-duty plastic bag. Seal securely, snip off one corner and gently squeeze to write words or form designs. Alternatively, use a pastry bag fitted with a plain tip with a small opening.

Stenciled designs
Cut out the desired design from a piece of paper and place the paper on top of the cake. Put confectioners' (icing) sugar or cocoa in a small sieve, hold the sieve over the cake and tap gently . . .

. . . until the cutouts are evenly coated. Then carefully lift off the paper, leaving the design stenciled on top.

Whipped cream rosettes
Fit a pastry bag with a star tip. Fill the bag half-full with whipped cream and gently squeeze to form rosettes such as those on the heavenly light cupcakes (page 57) and frozen chocolate dream (page 33). Rosettes should be made just before serving.

Chocolate curls
For wide chocolate curls such as those shown on pages 33 and 81, slightly soften a block of chocolate (a hand-held hair-dryer on the low setting helps). Then draw a vegetable peeler along the slightly softened edge. You may have to experiment with the temp-erature of the chocolate to get it right.

Chocolate shavings
For thin shavings such as those shown on page 92, lightly draw a vegetable peeler across a block of chocolate at cool room temperature.

Grating fine curls
For fine chocolate curls as shown on page 34, use a block of chocolate that has been stored in a cool place; the chocolate must be firm. Draw the chocolate over the holes on a hand-held grater to form delicate shreds of whatever size you prefer.

White Chocolate Cream

This topping, which has the consistency of soft cream cheese, must be made at least 4 hours in advance of using, so it can set up. It will keep for a week in the refrigerator or can be frozen for up to 6 months. Use it on top of a slice of plain chocolate cake such as bête noire (recipe on page 102), or spoon it over chocolate mousse, pudding or brownies, to turn a simple dessert into a fancy one. It is also delicious warmed and spooned over fresh fruit.

1 cup (8 fl oz/250 ml) heavy (double) cream
12 oz (375 g) best-quality white chocolate, chopped
  (2⅓ cups)
¼–⅓ cup (2–3 fl oz/60–80 ml) bourbon whiskey

Gently warm the cream in a small saucepan over medium heat until small bubbles begin to appear at the edges. Remove from the heat and stir in the chocolate until the mixture is smooth and the chocolate has melted completely. Do not stir so vigorously that bubbles form.

  Alternatively, place the chocolate in a food processor fitted with the metal blade or in a blender. Pour the hot cream over the chocolate and allow to sit for 15 seconds. With the pusher or lid in place to prevent splattering, process or blend until smooth.

  Add the bourbon to taste and process briefly. If there are any visible lumps, strain the mixture through a fine-mesh sieve. Before using, let cool, cover and chill for at least 4 hours, or until it no longer flows.

Makes about 3 cups (24 fl oz/750 ml)

Chocolate Ganache

This special yet simple combination of cream and chocolate can be used many ways. It can be flavored with 1 or 2 tablespoons Grand Marnier, framboise, kirsch or your favorite liqueur and served warm, as a sauce to accompany almost any dessert. At room temperature, pour over a cake to form the perfect shiny glaze. Ganache will keep in a covered container in the refrigerator for up to 1 month, or frozen for up to 6 months. To reheat, warm the sauce in a small heatproof bowl set over a pan of hot water or in a microwave on full power for 20–30 seconds.

1 cup (8 fl oz/250 ml) heavy (double) cream
10 oz (315 g) semisweet or bittersweet chocolate, chopped
  (2 cups)

Gently warm the cream in a small saucepan over medium heat until small bubbles begin to appear at the edges. Remove from the heat and stir in the chocolate until the mixture is smooth and the chocolate has melted completely. Do not stir so vigorously that bubbles form.

  Alternatively, place the chocolate in a food processor fitted with the metal blade or in a blender. Pour the hot cream over the chocolate and allow to sit for 15 seconds. With the pusher or lid in place to prevent splattering, process or blend until smooth.

  If there are any visible lumps, strain the mixture through a fine-mesh sieve.

*Makes about 3 cups
(24 fl oz/750 ml)*

White Chocolate Cream

Chocolate Ganache

Chocolate Whipped Cream

You may make this chocolatey whipped cream as much as 4 hours in advance. Spoon it into a fine-mesh strainer placed over a bowl, cover with plastic wrap and refrigerate until ready to use. The whipped cream will not be as light and fluffy, but it will still be fine. Any liquid it releases will drain into the bowl and will not cause the whipped cream to become runny. Once the whipped cream is added to a dessert, serve immediately.

2 cups (16 fl oz/500 ml) heavy (double) cream, chilled
1 cup (3–4 oz/90–125 g) confectioners' (icing) sugar, sifted before measuring
½ cup (1½ oz/45 g) unsweetened cocoa, sifted before measuring

Using a chilled metal bowl and chilled beaters, whip the cream for a few minutes until it just starts to thicken. Add the sifted sugar and sifted cocoa and continue beating until thick enough to hold firm peaks.

Take care not to overbeat or the cream will turn to butter.

Makes about 4 cups (32 fl oz/1 l)

Chocolate Coffee Sauce

Vary this recipe by adding 2 tablespoons of your favorite liqueur in place of the coffee. Some suggested substitutions include Grand Marnier, framboise, poire Williams, Kahlúa and amaretto. Serve it on a slice of bête noire (recipe on page 102), over vanilla or coffee ice cream, or with poached pears (page 22). This sauce will keep refrigerated for up to 1 month and frozen for up to 6 months.

1 cup (8 fl oz/250 ml) heavy (double) cream
2 tablespoons instant espresso powder
10 oz (315 g) semisweet or bittersweet chocolate, chopped (2 cups)

Gently warm the cream in a small saucepan over medium heat until small bubbles begin to appear at the edges. Add the espresso powder and stir until dissolved. Remove from the heat and stir in the chocolate until the mixture is smooth and the chocolate has melted completely.

Alternatively, place the chocolate in a food processor fitted with the metal blade or in a blender. Pour in the hot cream mixture. With the pusher or lid in place to prevent splattering, process or blend until smooth.

If there are any visible lumps, strain the mixture through a fine-mesh sieve.

Makes about 3 cups (24 fl oz/750 ml)

Chocolate Whipped Cream

Chocolate Coffee Sauce

13

Chocolate Fudge Sauce

Use this fudge sauce to make brownies à la mode with vanilla or coffee ice cream and whipped cream. The sauce will keep for several weeks in a covered container in the refrigerator. Soften it for serving by placing the container in a pan of hot water or in the microwave. To reheat until hot, place the sauce in a small metal bowl set in a pan of gently simmering water, or in a microwave set on high for 15–20 seconds, stirring at the midpoint.

2 cups (16 fl oz/500 ml) heavy (double) cream
½ cup (3 oz/90 g) firmly packed dark brown sugar
8 oz (250 g) bittersweet chocolate, chopped (1⅔ cups)
2 oz (60 g) unsweetened chocolate, chopped
  (rounded ⅓ cup)
3 tablespoons unsalted butter, cut into small pieces
2–3 tablespoons rum, preferably dark (optional)

*P*lace the cream in a large saucepan and bring to a boil. Watch carefully as it can easily boil over the sides. Reduce the heat to a simmer and cook until reduced by half. This will take 15–20 minutes.

  Stir in the brown sugar and heat, stirring, until dissolved. Remove from the heat and add the bittersweet and unsweetened chocolate and the butter, stirring until they melt and the mixture is smooth. Stir in the rum, if desired.

*Makes about 3½ cups
(28 fl oz/875 ml)*

Raspberry Sauce

Use this versatile sauce to dress up a variety of desserts: Spoon a little on a plate before you place a piece of cake— especially cheesecake—on it, or drizzle it over steamed chocolate pudding (recipe on page 51) or poached pears (page 22). For a slightly stronger flavor, add 2 tablespoons raspberry preserves or a few drops of fresh lemon juice. This sauce will keep for up to 2 weeks in the refrigerator and can be frozen for up to 6 months.

2½ cups (10 oz/315 g) fresh raspberries or thawed,
  frozen unsweetened raspberries
½ cup (4 oz/125 g) superfine (castor) sugar
¼ cup (2 fl oz/60 ml) framboise or other raspberry-
  flavored liqueur, optional

*P*lace the raspberries, sugar and liqueur, if desired, in a blender or in a food processor fitted with the metal blade. Purée until smooth. If a seedless sauce is desired, pass the purée through a sieve.

Makes about 3 cups (24 fl oz/750 ml)

Raspberry Sauce

Chocolate Fudge Sauce

Chocolate Crumb Crust

Use this quick-and-easy crust to line a pie plate or a thoroughly greased springform pan. The best chocolate cookies for making this crust are Nabisco-brand Famous Chocolate Wafers, available at most supermarkets.

1 package (7 oz/210 g) chocolate cookie wafers (*see note*)
¼ cup (2 oz/60 g) sugar
⅓ cup (3 oz/90 g) butter, preferably unsalted, melted

Position a rack in the middle of an oven and preheat the oven to 450°F (230°C). Select a 9- or 10-inch (23- or 25-cm) pie plate (preferably glass) or springform pan. If using a springform pan, carefully butter the sides and bottom.

Crush the wafers into fine crumbs: Break into pieces, place in a food processor fitted with the metal blade and process finely. Or place the wafers in a heavy-duty plastic bag and crush them with a rolling pin. (You will have about 3 cups.)

In a mixing bowl combine the crumbs, sugar and butter and, using a fork, mix completely. Press the crumb mixture onto the bottom and sides of the plate or pan. In the springform pan the crumb coating will come only halfway up the sides and will be slightly uneven, which is fine. Bake for 5 minutes, let cool, cover and chill well before filling.

Makes one 9- or 10-inch (23- or 25-cm) pie crust

Homemade Chocolate Syrup

You'll never have to rely on store-bought chocolate syrup again! Use the syrup hot, or let cool, cover and chill before serving. Spoon it over French vanilla ice cream or stir it into a glass of cold milk. This will keep for several weeks in the refrigerator. To make mint-flavored chocolate syrup, substitute ½ teaspoon mint extract (essence) for the vanilla.

4 oz (125 g) unsweetened chocolate, chopped
  (scant 1 cup)
¾ cup (6 fl oz/180 ml) water, boiling
1¼ cups (10 oz/310 g) sugar
1 teaspoon vanilla extract (essence)

Combine the chocolate and boiling water in a saucepan. Place over medium-low heat and stir until the chocolate melts completely. Stir in the sugar and raise the heat so that the mixture barely simmers. Cook, stirring constantly, for 5 minutes. Remove from the heat and stir in the vanilla.

Makes 1½ cups (12 fl oz/375 ml)

Homemade Chocolate Syrup

Chocolate Crumb Crust

Chocolate Champagne Truffles

1 cup (8 fl oz/250 ml) heavy (double) cream
12 oz (375 g) best-quality bittersweet chocolate, chopped (2⅓ cups)
3–4 tablespoons (2 fl oz/60 ml) Marc de Champagne
⅓ cup (1½ oz/45 g) unsweetened cocoa

These are the ultimate in chocolate luxury. The secret ingredient is a liqueur called Marc de Champagne, an eau-de-vie made from Champagne grapes, available in fine wine shops. Or substitute any fine Cognac. Use the best bittersweet chocolate you can find. My favorite choice for this recipe is Côte d'Or extra bittersweet.

Gently warm the cream in a saucepan over medium heat until small bubbles begin to appear along the pan's edges. Place the chocolate in a food processor fitted with the metal blade or in a blender. Pour the hot cream over the chocolate and allow to sit for 15 seconds. With the pusher or lid in place to prevent splattering, process or blend until smooth. Add the liqueur to taste and mix briefly. Pour the mixture into a shallow pan, cover with plastic wrap and chill until very firm, about 3 hours.

Place the cocoa in a shallow bowl or saucer. To form each truffle: Using a teaspoon scoop up a 1-inch (2.5-cm) piece of the mixture. With cool fingers, form the mixture into an irregularly shaped ball, then drop the ball into the cocoa and turn to coat it completely. Transfer to a plate. If your fingers are not cool, drop the mixture directly into the cocoa and quickly form it into a ball as you coat it.

Store for up to 2 weeks in a covered container in the refrigerator; remove 30 minutes before serving. Or freeze for up to 4 months in a tightly sealed container; defrost in the container.

Makes about 30 truffles

Chocolate-Dipped Fruits and Nut Clusters

8 oz (250 g) sweet, semisweet or
  bittersweet chocolate, very finely
  chopped (1⅔ cups)
12–16 pieces assorted fresh or dried
  fruits, or 1½ cups (6–8 oz/185–250 g)
  unsalted whole nuts
12–16 fluted paper candy cups

Whole strawberries, sliced bananas and peaches, seedless orange sections and raspberry clusters are all good for dipping; be sure to dry the berries carefully after rinsing. Also consider dried apricots, oranges, pears and apples and candied ginger slices.

Place the chocolate in a 1-qt (1-l) freezer-strength plastic bag with a self-sealing top. Force out excess air and seal. Place a 2-qt (2-l) saucepan in the sink and fill with hot tap water. With the water running, insert an instant-read thermometer into the water. When it registers 118°F (48°C), turn off the water and submerge the bag (you'll have to push it down). Do not allow the water temperature to rise above 118°F (48°C). It will take about 20 minutes to melt completely; press against the bag to dissolve any lumps. Dry the bag thoroughly. Snip off one bottom corner of the bag.

For fresh fruits, squeeze the chocolate into a small bowl. Dip each piece of fruit about halfway into the chocolate and place in a paper cup. Refrigerate until the chocolate hardens, about 15 minutes, or for up to 2 hours. Eat within 2 hours of dipping.

For dried fruits, proceed as for fresh fruits, but refrigerate only until the chocolate hardens. For nut clusters, line up the paper cups and place several nuts in each one. Squeeze the chocolate over the nuts and refrigerate until it hardens, about 15 minutes. Store covered at room temperature for several weeks.

Makes about 1 cup (8 fl oz/250 ml) dipping chocolate, enough for 12–16 confections

Chocolate Raspberry Truffles

6 tablespoons (3 oz/90 g) unsalted
  butter
8 oz (250 g) semisweet or bittersweet
  chocolate, chopped (1⅔ cups)
½ cup (5 oz/155 g) best-quality
  seedless raspberry jam
3 tablespoons framboise or other
  raspberry-flavored liqueur or crème
  de cassis
⅓ cup (3 oz/90 g) sugar

There is something magical about the combination of chocolate and raspberry. In these elegant truffles, the raspberry flavor comes from raspberry preserves and a small amount of liqueur. If you can find a high-quality raspberry flavoring or essence, try adding a small amount (start with ¼ teaspoon). The truffles are also good coated in cocoa powder. Garnish the serving plate with fresh raspberries, if you like.

Place the butter and chocolate in a heatproof bowl or the top pan of a double boiler. Set over a pan of gently simmering water but not touching the water. Stir until melted and smooth. Remove from the heat and stir in the jam and liqueur. Pour the mixture into a shallow pan, cover with plastic wrap and chill until very firm, about 3 hours.

Place the sugar in a shallow bowl or saucer. To form each truffle: Using a teaspoon scoop up a 1-inch (2.5-cm) piece of the mixture. With cool fingers, form the mixture into an irregularly shaped or smooth ball, then drop the ball into the sugar and turn to coat it completely. Transfer to a plate. If your fingers are not cool, drop the mixture directly into the sugar and quickly form it into a ball as you coat it.

Store for up to 2 weeks in a covered container in the refrigerator; remove 30 minutes before serving. Or freeze for up to 4 months in a tightly sealed container; defrost in the container.

Makes about 36 truffles

Poached Pears with Chocolate Sauce

6 slightly underripe large Bartlett, Comice or Anjou pears
2 cups (16 fl oz/500 ml) sweet white wine or 1 cup (8 fl oz/250 ml) each white grape juice and water
6 whole cloves
⅔ cup (5 oz/155 g) firmly packed brown sugar
peel of 1 orange, cut into several strips
3 cups (24 fl oz/750 ml) white chocolate cream (*recipe on page 12*) or chocolate ganache (*page 12*), heated to the consistency of very thick cream

These delicate poached pears also look and taste wonderful served with 1½ cups (12 fl oz/375 ml) each chocolate ganache and raspberry sauce or white chocolate cream and chocolate ganache (recipes on pages 12–14). Or spoon chocolate coffee sauce (page 13) on top. A good Riesling, fruit wine or apple cider can be used for the sweet white wine.

Select a heavy pan (preferably enamelware) with a tight-fitting lid that can accommodate all the pears placed upright. Using a sharp paring knife, peel off the skin, then slice off the very bottom of each pear so it will stand straight. Using an apple corer or other sharp-edged tool, scoop out the seeds and part of the core from the bottom of each pear.

Add the wine or grape juice and water, cloves, brown sugar and the orange peel to the pan. Stir to dissolve the sugar slightly, then add the pears. Do not worry that the pears are not covered by the liquid. Cover and place over medium heat until the liquid comes to a gentle simmer. Continue simmering until a sharp knife inserted in the side of the pears goes in easily, 20–30 minutes. The cooking time will depend upon the type, size and ripeness of the pears; do not overcook or they will fall apart.

Using a slotted spoon gently transfer the pears to a large serving dish or to individual dishes. Cool to room temperature. Blot with paper towels to remove excess moisture. Spoon a pool of the sauce around each pear.

Serves 6

Chocolate Fudge Squares

5 oz (155 g) unsweetened chocolate,
  chopped (1 cup)
½ cup (4 oz/125 g) unsalted butter
½ cup (4 oz/125 g) vegetable
  shortening
4 extra-large eggs
2 cups (1 lb/500 g) sugar
1 cup (4 oz/125 g) all-purpose (plain)
  flour, sifted before measuring

This fudgy sweet has a texture and a taste akin to truffles but is made in a single pan and carved into small squares. Don't forget to cut into squares while it is still hot.

Position a rack in the middle of an oven and preheat the oven to 325°F (165°C). Grease a 9-inch (23-cm) square baking pan.

Place the chocolate, butter and shortening in a heatproof bowl or the top pan of a double boiler. Set over a pan of gently simmering water but not touching the water. Stir until melted and smooth. Set aside to cool slightly.

Combine the eggs and sugar in a bowl. Using a whisk or an electric mixer set on medium speed, beat until thick and light colored, 5–10 minutes. Using a rubber spatula fold in the cooled chocolate and then the sifted flour, mixing only until the ingredients are incorporated.

Pour into the prepared pan and bake until the top looks dry and feels firm to the touch, 45 minutes. Cut into 1½-inch (4-cm) squares while still hot; cool before serving.

Makes 36 squares

Jody Adams' Dark and White Chocolate Truffles

8 oz (250 g) bittersweet chocolate, chopped (1⅔ cups)

6 tablespoons (3 oz/90 g) unsalted butter, at room temperature

1 tablespoon rum, preferably dark

⅔ cup (2 oz/60 g) toasted pecans, finely chopped

3 oz (90 g) white chocolate, finely chopped (scant ⅔ cup)

⅓ cup (1½ oz/45 g) unsweetened cocoa

Jody Adams is the chef and creative genius at Michela's restaurant in Cambridge, Massachusetts. This is her inspired recipe for a fabulous truffle.

Place the bittersweet chocolate in a small heatproof bowl or the top pan of a double boiler. Set over a pan of gently simmering water but not touching the water. Stir until smooth, then add the butter and stir until shiny and smooth. Stir in the rum, pour into a shallow pan, cover with plastic wrap and chill until cool but still soft, 1–1½ hours.

Fold in the pecans and white chocolate and chill until firmly set, about 2 hours.

Place the cocoa in a shallow bowl or saucer. To form each truffle: Using a teaspoon scoop up a 1-inch (2.5-cm) piece of the mixture. With cool fingers, form the mixture into an irregularly shaped ball, then drop the ball into the cocoa and turn to coat it completely. Transfer to a plate. If your fingers are not cool, drop the mixture directly into the cocoa and quickly form it into a ball as you coat it.

Store for up to 2 weeks in a covered container in the refrigerator; remove 30 minutes before serving. Or freeze for up to 4 months in a tightly sealed container; defrost in the container.

Makes about 20 truffles

Ginger Chocolate Chunk Ice Cream

1 pt (16 fl oz/500 ml) best-quality
   vanilla ice cream
⅓ cup (2 oz/60 g) candied ginger,
   finely chopped, plus extra for
   garnish
½ cup (2½ oz/75 g) semisweet
   chocolate chips or 3 oz (90 g)
   bittersweet chocolate, coarsely
   chopped
3 cups (24 fl oz/750 ml) chocolate
   fudge sauce, heated (*recipe on
   page 14*)

If you don't own an ice cream maker, you can customize store-bought ice cream to make your own delicious flavors. Be sure to use top-quality ice cream, or the ice cream will deflate when you add the mix-ins.

Soften the ice cream by setting it out at room temperature, about 30 minutes. Alternatively, place it in a microwave oven set on high for 15 seconds; if it does not soften, repeat.

Scoop the ice cream into a metal mixing bowl. Using a large spoon or an electric mixer set on medium speed, beat the ginger and chocolate into the ice cream. Scoop the ice cream into a container, cover and refreeze.

Serve with the fudge sauce and garnish with candied ginger.

Serves 4–6

Frozen Chocolate Dream

chocolate crumb crust *(recipe on page 15)*

8 oz (250 g) semisweet or bittersweet chocolate, chopped (1⅔ cups)

6 oz (185 g) cream cheese, softened

⅔ cup (5 oz/155 g) sugar

1 teaspoon vanilla extract (essence)

½ cup (4 fl oz/125 ml) milk

2 cups (16 fl oz/500 ml) heavy (double) cream, whipped

1 thick square semisweet or bittersweet chocolate for topping, optional

This impressive and magnificently delicious creation is an easy make-ahead dessert—the perfect finish to a fancy dinner party or special birthday celebration. If you like, decorate the top with whipped cream rosettes (see page 11).

Prepare the crust in a 10-inch (25-cm) pie plate. Prebake as directed, then cool and chill.

Place the chocolate in a small heatproof bowl or the top pan of a double boiler. Set over a pan of gently simmering water but not touching the water. Stir until melted and smooth, then remove from the heat and cool to lukewarm.

Combine the cream cheese, sugar, vanilla and milk in a bowl. Using an electric mixer set on medium speed (or a wooden spoon if the cream cheese is soft enough), beat until thoroughly mixed. Using a rubber spatula, gently fold in the whipped cream and cooled chocolate, taking care not to deflate the mixture.

Pour and scrape the mixture into the prepared crust, smoothing the top with a rubber spatula. Cover with aluminum foil and freeze for at least 4 hours or overnight.

Using a vegetable peeler, shave chocolate curls from the thick square of chocolate, if desired, and arrange on top.

Makes one 10-inch (25-cm) pie; serves 8

Frozen Espresso Mousse

8 oz (250 g) bittersweet or semisweet
   chocolate, chopped (1⅔ cups)
½ cup (4 fl oz/125 ml) double-
   strength brewed espresso
3 tablespoons crème de cacao
2 cups (16 fl oz/500 ml) heavy
   (double) cream, chilled
½ cup (4 oz/125 g) sugar
1 thick square semisweet or
   bittersweet chocolate for topping
3 cups (24 fl oz/750 ml) chocolate
   coffee sauce *(recipe on page 13)*

You couldn't ask for an easier, more delicious and elegant dessert. You can use espresso made from instant espresso powder or brewed with an espresso machine. An attractive way to present this is in a soufflé dish.

Combine the chocolate and espresso in a small heatproof bowl or the top pan of a double boiler. Set over a pan of gently simmering water but not touching the water. Stir until melted and smooth. Remove from the heat and cool to lukewarm. Stir in the crème de cacao.

Using chilled beaters and a chilled bowl, whip together the cream and sugar until stiff peaks form. Using a rubber spatula gently fold the whipped cream into the cooled chocolate mixture.

Pour and scrape the mixture into a 1½-qt (48-fl oz/1.5-l) serving dish. Cover with aluminum foil and freeze for at least 4 hours or as long as overnight.

Using a metal or plastic grater, grate the square of chocolate over the top of the mousse. Serve with the chocolate coffee sauce.

Serves 8

Chocolate Ice Cream Roll

8 extra-large eggs, separated and at room temperature

1 cup (8 oz/250 g) sugar

⅓ cup (1½ oz/45 g) unsweetened cocoa (not Dutch-process type), sifted after measuring, plus extra for dusting

2 tablespoons all-purpose (plain) flour

1 qt (1 l) best-quality ice cream of choice

3 cups (24 fl oz/750 ml) chocolate fudge sauce (*recipe on page 14*)

Fill this egg-rich chocolate roll with your favorite ice cream.

Position a rack in the middle of an oven and preheat the oven to 350°F (180°C). Line an 11½-by-17-inch (29-by-43-cm) jelly-roll pan with parchment paper or waxed paper.

Combine the egg yolks and half of the sugar in a bowl. Using an electric mixer set on high speed, beat until thick and pale. Reduce the speed to low, add the cocoa and flour and beat until mixed. In another bowl and with clean beaters, beat the egg whites with the remaining sugar until soft peaks form. Using a rubber spatula, gently fold into the cocoa mixture.

Spread in the pan and smooth the top. Bake until the top looks dry and feels spongy, 9–12 minutes; turn the pan 180 degrees halfway through baking. Remove from the oven and cover loosely with a lightly dampened towel until cool.

Meanwhile, soften the ice cream slightly at room temperature, about 30 minutes. Alternatively, place in a microwave oven set on high for 15 seconds; repeat if needed.

Run a knife around the cake's edges. Dust the top with cocoa. Lay 2 sheets of plastic wrap over the top to extend slightly beyond the pan edges. Place a baking sheet on top and invert the pan. Lift off the pan and the paper. Trim the cake to even the edges.

Spread the ice cream to within 1 inch (2.5 cm) of the edges. With the aid of the plastic wrap and starting from a long side, roll up to form a long, firm roll. Wrap it with the plastic wrap and then aluminum foil. Freeze for at least 2 hours or for up to 1 month. To serve, cut into slices. Pass the fudge sauce.

Serves 10–12

Chocolate Mandarin Ice Cream

4 egg yolks
⅔ cup (5 oz/155 g) firmly packed
   light brown sugar
2 tablespoons unsweetened cocoa
1 cup (8 fl oz/250 ml) heavy (double)
   cream
¼ cup (2 fl oz/60 ml) Grand Marnier
   or other orange-flavored liqueur
6 oz (180 g) best-quality milk
   chocolate, finely chopped (1⅓ cups)
finely grated zest of 1 orange

*The delicious combination of milk chocolate and orange gives this
rich ice cream a sophisticated taste. Grate only the orange-colored
part of the orange peel; the white portion imparts a bitter taste.
You will need an ice cream maker for this recipe.*

Combine the egg yolks, brown sugar and cocoa in a large
bowl. Using either a whisk or an electric mixer set on
medium speed, beat until light and slightly thickened,
3–4 minutes.

Gently warm the cream in a heavy-bottomed, 1-qt (1-l)
saucepan over medium heat until small bubbles begin to
appear at the edges. Add ¼ cup (2 fl oz/60 ml) of the hot
cream to the egg mixture, stirring steadily. Then stir the egg
mixture into the remaining hot cream. Cook over medium
heat, stirring constantly and scraping the bottom and sides
of the pan, until thick enough to coat the back of the spoon,
about 5 minutes. Do not allow the mixture to boil or it will
curdle. Strain the mixture through a fine-mesh sieve into a
metal bowl. Stir in the liqueur, cover and refrigerate to cool
completely.

Stir in the chocolate and orange zest and pour into an ice
cream maker. Freeze according to the manufacturer's
directions. Store in a tightly covered container in the freezer
for up to 1 week.

Makes 1½ pt (24 fl oz/750 ml); serves 4–6

Chocolate Sorbet

2 cups (16 fl oz/500 ml) water

1¼ cups (8 oz/250 g) superfine (castor) sugar

8 oz (250 g) unsweetened chocolate, chopped (1⅔ cups)

You don't need an ice cream maker to prepare this light yet intensely flavored dessert; your freezer will work just fine. For a special occasion, garnish with candied violets.

Combine the water and sugar in a small saucepan and bring to a boil over medium heat, stirring until the sugar dissolves completely. Cool to room temperature.

Place the chocolate in a small heatproof bowl or the top pan of a double boiler. Set over a pan of gently simmering water but not touching the water. Stir until melted and smooth, then stir into the cooled sugar syrup.

Pour into an ice cream maker and freeze according to the manufacturer's directions. Alternatively, pour into a shallow metal bowl, place in a freezer and freeze until frozen, stirring with a fork every hour or so to break up the ice crystals.

To serve, scoop into individual dishes.

Makes 1½ pt (24 fl oz/750 ml); serves 4

Fast Fondue

⅔ cup (5 fl oz/160 ml) dark corn
    syrup
½ cup (4 fl oz/125 ml) heavy (double)
    cream
9 oz (280 g) semisweet chocolate,
    chopped (1¾ cups)
assorted sliced fresh fruits such as
    apples, peaches, pears, strawberries,
    nectarines or pineapple

Looking for a quick chocolate fix? This instant yet elegant dessert is the answer. Just heat and mix. All you need to add is the fruit. The combination of warm chocolate and fruit is simply heavenly. A fondue pot is an excellent way to keep the chocolate warm at the table.

*I*n a saucepan over medium heat, bring the corn syrup and cream to a gentle boil. Remove from the heat and add the chocolate, stirring until completely melted.

Arrange the fruits on a platter. Pass toothpicks or skewers to spear the fruits for dipping into the warm chocolate.

Makes 1½ cups (12 fl oz/375 ml); serves 4

Denver Chocolate Pudding Cake

2 oz (60 g) unsweetened chocolate, chopped (rounded ⅓ cup)

½ cup (4 oz/125 g) unsalted butter, at room temperature

1⅓ cups (10 oz/310 g) granulated sugar

1 cup (4 oz/125 g) all-purpose (plain) flour, sifted before measuring

1½ teaspoons baking powder

½ teaspoon salt

½ cup (4 fl oz/125 ml) milk

2 teaspoons vanilla extract (essence)

½ cup (3 oz/90 g) firmly packed dark brown sugar

3 rounded tablespoons unsweetened cocoa

1½ cups (12 fl oz/375 ml) water, boiling

There are many versions of this delectable dessert, which comes out of the oven with the cake on the top and the sauce on the bottom. It is best slightly cooled from the oven, but is fine chilled as well. Serve with coffee or vanilla ice cream or whipped cream.

Position a rack in the middle of an oven; preheat the oven to 350°F (180°C). Butter a 9-inch (23-cm) square baking pan.

Place the chocolate in a small heatproof bowl or the top pan of a double boiler. Set over a pan of gently simmering water but not touching the water. Stir until melted and smooth. Let cool slightly.

Combine the butter and half of the granulated sugar in a bowl. Using a whisk or an electric mixer set on high speed, beat until light and fluffy, 7–8 minutes with the whisk or 4–5 minutes with the mixer. Sift together the sifted flour, baking powder and salt onto the butter mixture and then add the milk. Stir with the whisk or the mixer on low speed until well mixed. Using a rubber spatula, fold in the chocolate and 1 teaspoon of the vanilla. Spread the mixture evenly in the prepared pan.

In the same bowl (no need to wash it if you have scraped it clean), stir together the remaining granulated sugar, the brown sugar and cocoa. Sprinkle over the batter in the pan. Add the remaining 1 teaspoon vanilla to the boiling water and pour slowly over the batter so as not to disturb it too much. Bake until the top is firm, about 1 hour. Let cool slightly.

To serve, cut into squares. Spoon some of the sauce from the pan bottom over each serving.

Serves 8

Chocolate Crème Brûlée

5½ cups (44 fl oz/1.3 l) heavy
  (double) cream
½ cup (4 oz/125 g) granulated sugar
8 oz (250 g) bittersweet chocolate,
  chopped (1⅔ cups)
2 oz (60 g) unsweetened chocolate,
  chopped (rounded ⅓ cup)
8 extra-large egg yolks

FOR THE TOPPING:
1⅓ cups (10 oz/315 g) firmly packed
  brown sugar
¼ cup (2 fl oz/60 ml) water, boiling

*If you don't have individual soufflé dishes or ramekins, make one
large crème brûlée in an ovenproof baking dish.*

Position a rack in the lower third of an oven (not the
bottom) and preheat the oven to 350°F (180°C). Set eight
1-cup (8-fl oz/250-ml) ovenproof ramekins or individual
soufflé dishes in a roasting pan or jelly-roll pan with at least
1-inch (2.5-cm) sides. Do not allow the cups to touch.

Combine the cream and granulated sugar in a large
heatproof bowl or the top pan of a double boiler. Set over
gently simmering water but not touching the water. Stir until
the sugar dissolves. Add both chocolates and stir until they
melt. Set aside to cool slightly.

Place the egg yolks in a bowl. Using a whisk or an electric
mixer set on high speed, beat until light and double in
volume, 7–10 minutes with a whisk or about 5 minutes
with a mixer. Mix in the chocolate. Divide the mixture
evenly among the dishes. Place the pan in the oven and
pour in hot water to reach halfway up its sides. Bake until
set and a knife inserted in the center comes out clean, about
50 minutes. Remove the cups from the pan and let cool for
20 minutes, then cover and chill for at least 2 hours.

Position the broiler (griller) rack in the highest position
and preheat the broiler. To make the topping, stir together
the brown sugar and boiling water. Using a teaspoon spread
2 tablespoons of the paste over each chilled custard.

Broil (grill) until the tops bubble and turn deep brown.
Refrigerate until serving, but no longer than 24 hours.

Serves 8

Steamed Chocolate Pudding

4 oz (125 g) semisweet or bittersweet
  chocolate, chopped (scant 1 cup)
½ cup (4 oz/125 g) unsalted butter
1 extra-large egg
½ cup (4 oz/125 g) sugar
1 cup (4 oz/125 g) all-purpose (plain)
  flour, sifted before measuring
1½ teaspoons baking powder
½ cup (4 fl oz/125 ml) milk
1 tablespoon vanilla extract (essence)

*Steamed pudding is a traditional winter holiday dessert. It is best
made in a traditional pudding mold with a watertight lid. Try
serving it hot with a dollop of white chocolate cream (recipe on
page 12), or at room temperature with soft whipped cream or
raspberry sauce (page 14).*

Generously butter a 1-qt (1-l) heatproof mold.

Place the chocolate and butter in a heatproof bowl or the
top pan of a double boiler. Set over a pan of gently simmering water but not touching the water. Stir until melted and
smooth. Remove from the heat and let cool slightly.

In a small bowl combine the egg and sugar and stir with a
fork just to mix. Stir the egg mixture into the chocolate.

Sift together the sifted flour and the baking powder onto
the chocolate mixture. Gently fold the flour mixture into the
chocolate mixture, mixing just until incorporated. Stir in the
milk and vanilla. Pour and scrape the mixture into the
prepared mold. Cover tightly with aluminum foil and tie in
place with string.

Set the mold on a wire rack in a pot or kettle large enough
to accommodate it comfortably. Pour in hot water to reach
halfway up the sides of the mold. Cover the pot and place
over medium heat until the water starts to simmer, then
lower the heat so the water is barely simmering. Steam until
the pudding is set, about 1½ hours. Add hot water to the
pot as needed to maintain the water level.

Invert the pudding onto a serving plate and lift off the
mold. Serve hot or at room temperature.

Serves 6–8

Chocolate Pudding

2½ cups (20 fl oz/625 ml) milk

4 extra-large egg yolks

¾ cup (6 oz/180 g) sugar

¼ cup (1½ oz/45 g) all-purpose (plain) flour

3 tablespoons cornstarch (cornflour)

4 oz (125 g) semisweet or bittersweet chocolate, chopped (scant 1 cup)

2 oz (60 g) unsweetened chocolate, chopped (rounded ⅓ cup)

1 teaspoon vanilla extract (essence)

1 cup (8 fl oz/250 ml) heavy (double) cream, whipped

Serve this pudding in individual dishes or use it to fill a 9-inch (23-cm) prebaked chocolate crumb crust (recipe on page 15) and top it with whipped cream for a chocolate cream pie. In either case, the rewards of from-scratch chocolate pudding will be evident. The key to success is to use moderate heat and to whisk constantly, scraping the pan bottom carefully.

*P*our all but about 2 tablespoons of the milk into a saucepan and warm gently over medium heat until small bubbles begin to appear at the pan's edges.

Meanwhile, combine the egg yolks, sugar, flour and cornstarch in a bowl. Stir in the remaining 2 tablespoons milk to form a paste. Using a whisk, vigorously stir the hot milk into the egg mixture. Then pour the milk-egg mixture back into the pan. Place over medium-low heat and bring to a boil, whisking constantly and carefully scraping the sides and bottom of the pan to prevent scorching. When the mixture reaches a boil, continue whisking constantly for 1 full minute.

Remove from the heat and add the chocolates and vanilla extract, whisking continuously until the chocolates melt and the mixture is smooth.

Pour into 8 individual dishes and let cool. Cover with plastic wrap and refrigerate until completely chilled. Top with the whipped cream just before serving.

Serves 8

Chocolate Decadence

1 lb (500 g) semisweet or bittersweet
  chocolate, chopped (scant 3 cups)
½ cup plus 2 tablespoons (5 oz/150 g)
  unsalted butter, at room temperature
4 extra-large eggs, at room
  temperature
1 tablespoon sugar
1 tablespoon all-purpose (plain) flour
3 cups (24 fl oz/750 ml) raspberry
  sauce *(recipe on page 14)*
1 cup (8 fl oz/250 ml) heavy (double)
  cream, whipped

This fabulous dessert is a legend in its own time. Although many have claimed to be the creator, it was in fact developed at Narsai's restaurant in Berkeley, California, by chef Narsai David and pastry chef Janice Feuer. To be completely authentic you should use Ghirardelli sweet dark chocolate.

Position a rack in the middle of an oven and preheat the oven to 425°F (220°C). Butter an 8- or 9-inch (20- or 23-cm) layer cake pan or springform pan. Line the bottom with a circle of parchment paper or waxed paper cut to fit precisely. Butter the paper and dust with flour; tap out any excess.

  Place the chocolate and butter in a large heatproof bowl or the top pan of a double boiler. Set over a pan of gently simmering water but not touching the water. Stir occasionally until melted and combine completely. Remove from the heat and let cool slightly.

  Place the eggs and sugar in a bowl. Using an electric mixer set on high speed, beat until light, fluffy and tripled in volume, 5–10 minutes. Reduce the speed to low and beat in the flour. Using a rubber spatula fold one-third of the egg mixture into the chocolate to lighten it, then fold in the remaining egg mixture, taking care not to deflate the batter. Pour and scrape into the prepared pan and smooth the top.

  Bake for exactly 15 minutes. Let cool completely to room temperature. Do not refrigerate or the cake will stick to the pan. Invert onto a flat serving plate and peel off the paper. Cut into small wedges and serve each wedge atop the raspberry sauce. Top with whipped cream.

Makes one 8- or 9-inch (20- or 23-cm) cake; serves 10–12

Heavenly Light Cupcakes

4 oz (125 g) unsweetened chocolate, chopped (scant 1 cup)

6 tablespoons (3 oz/90 g) unsalted butter, at room temperature

3 extra-large whole eggs, lightly beaten, plus 3 extra-large egg whites

½ cup (4 oz/125 g) sugar

2 tablespoons all-purpose (plain) flour

1½ cups (12 fl oz/375 ml) chocolate whipped cream (*recipe on page 13*)

These cupcakes don't rise very high, but they are rich and heavenly light, hence their name. They are topped with a swirl of chocolate whipped cream, or you can pipe some cream inside: Prepare ½ recipe of the chocolate whipped cream and spoon it into a pastry bag fitted with a star tip. Gently push the tip into the top of the cupcake and squeeze a dab of cream inside.

Position a rack in the middle of an oven and preheat the oven to 350°F (180°C). Line 12 muffin-tin cups with fluted paper cups.

Place the chocolate and butter in a large heatproof bowl or the top pan of a double boiler. Set over a pan of gently simmering water but not touching the water. Stir until melted and smooth. Let cool for 5 minutes and then stir in the whole eggs, sugar and flour.

Meanwhile, place the egg whites in a separate bowl. Using an electric mixer set on high speed, beat until stiff and glossy but not dry. Using a rubber spatula fold the egg whites into the chocolate mixture. Spoon into the muffin cups, filling each cup only two-thirds full.

Bake until the tops look dry, 12–14 minutes. Transfer to a wire rack to cool completely before icing. Top each cupcake with some of the chocolate whipped cream. If refrigerating before serving, chill for no more than 6 hours.

Makes about 12 cupcakes

White Chocolate–Cherry Bars

2¼ cups (9 oz/280 g) all-purpose (plain) flour, sifted before measuring

1 teaspoon baking powder

½ teaspoon baking soda (bicarbonate of soda)

½ teaspoon salt

½ cup (4 oz/125 g) unsalted butter, at room temperature

⅔ cup (5 oz/155 g) firmly packed light brown sugar

½ cup (4 oz/125 g) granulated sugar

2 large eggs

1½ teaspoons almond extract (essence)

1 cup (5 oz/155 g) dried cherries

9 oz (280 g) white chocolate, coarsely chopped (scant 2 cups)

1 cup (4 oz/125 g) slivered blanched almonds

The tartness of dried cherries melds perfectly with white chocolate in these easy-to-make bars. Slivered almonds give them a delightful crunch. Dried cherries are available in specialty-food shops and health-food stores. If you cannot find them, substitute golden raisins.

Position a rack in the middle of an oven and preheat the oven to 350°F (180°C). Butter and flour a 9-by-13-inch (23-by-33-cm) baking dish.

Sift together the sifted flour, baking powder, baking soda and salt. Set aside.

Place the butter and both sugars in a large bowl. Using a whisk or an electric mixer set on medium speed, beat until light and fluffy, about 5 minutes with a whisk or 2–3 minutes with a mixer. Add the eggs one at a time, beating well after each addition, then add the almond extract. Add the flour mixture and carefully beat just until thoroughly combined. Stir in the cherries, white chocolate and almonds. Pour and scrape the batter into the prepared baking dish, smoothing the top with a rubber spatula.

Bake until the top is golden and the edges have just started to pull away from the sides, 35–45 minutes. Transfer to a wire rack and let cool completely, then cut into bars. Store in a covered container at room temperature for up to 1 week.

Makes 16–20 bars

Chocolate Chiffon Cake

¾ cup (6 fl oz/180 ml) water, boiling

½ cup (1½ oz/45 g) unsweetened cocoa (not Dutch-process type)

1¾ cups (7 oz/220 g) all-purpose (plain) flour, sifted before measuring

1¾ cups (14 oz/440 g) sugar

1 tablespoon baking powder

½ teaspoon salt

7 eggs, separated and at room temperature

½ cup (4 fl oz/125 ml) vegetable oil

2 teaspoons vanilla extract (essence)

½ teaspoon cream of tartar

strawberries, blueberries or kiwi fruit slices

Lighter than air, sweet as a kiss, this low-fat dessert is delicious topped with fresh fruit or a small dollop of whipped cream. For this recipe you will need a 10-inch (25-cm) tube pan; the type with a removable bottom makes it easier to get the cake out of the pan. Note that the oven temperature is raised during baking.

*P*osition a rack in the lower third of an oven (not on the bottom) and preheat the oven to 325°F (165°C).

Combine the boiling water and cocoa in a small bowl and stir to dissolve; set aside. Sift together the sifted flour, sugar, baking powder and salt into a mixing bowl. Add the cocoa mixture, egg yolks, oil and vanilla. Using a whisk or an electric mixer set on low, beat until thoroughly combined.

In a clean bowl using clean beaters, beat together the egg whites and cream of tartar until stiff and glossy but not dry. Using a rubber spatula, gently mix one-fourth of the whites into the chocolate mixture to lighten it, then fold in the remaining whites, taking care not to deflate the batter. Pour and scrape the batter into an ungreased 10-inch (25-cm) tube pan and smooth the top.

Bake for 55 minutes. Raise the oven temperature to 350°F (180°C) and continue baking until a toothpick comes out clean and dry, 10–15 minutes longer. Remove the cake from the oven and invert the pan (use a narrow-neck bottle to rest the tube section if the cake pan does not have supports). Let cool completely before removing. Top with the fruit.

Makes one 10-inch (25-cm) cake; serves 8–10

Macadamia Nut White Chocolate Chunk Cookies

1 cup (4 oz/125 g) plus 2 tablespoons all-purpose (plain) flour, sifted before measuring

½ teaspoon baking soda (bicarbonate of soda)

¼ teaspoon salt if using unsalted macadamia nuts

½ cup (4 oz/125 g) unsalted butter, at room temperature

½ cup (3 oz/90 g) firmly packed dark brown sugar

¼ cup (2 oz/60 g) granulated sugar

1 egg

1½ teaspoons vanilla extract (essence)

scant 2 cups (9 oz/280 g) white chocolate chips or 9 oz (280 g) white chocolate, coarsely chopped

1 cup (4 oz/125 g) macadamia nuts, each nut cut into 2 or 3 pieces

These crisp, buttery cookies combine two of the world's great flavors: white chocolate and macadamia nuts. If you can find only salted macadamia nuts, place them in a strainer and shake well to rid them of as much salt as possible. Substitute pistachio nuts for the macadamia nuts, if you like. Although these cookies will keep for 2 weeks, they are best when eaten within a few days.

*P*osition a rack in the middle of an oven and preheat the oven to 350°F (180°C). Butter 2 heavy-duty baking sheets.

Sift together the sifted flour, baking soda and salt (if using) into a mixing bowl. In a separate bowl, combine the butter and brown and white sugars. Using a whisk or an electric mixer set on high speed, beat until light and fluffy, 7–8 minutes with a whisk or about 5 minutes with a mixer. Beat in the egg and vanilla. Add the flour mixture, mixing only until combined. Stir in the white chocolate and nuts.

Using a tablespoon, scoop up balls of the dough and place them about 1 inch (2.5 cm) apart on the prepared baking sheets. There should be about 30 in all. Dip a fork into cool water and use to flatten the tops of the cookies slightly.

Bake the sheets of cookies, one at a time, until the cookie tops look dry and are beginning to brown, 10–12 minutes, turning the sheet 180 degrees midway through baking. Let cool on the sheet for 15 minutes, then transfer to a wire rack to cool completely. Store in a covered container at room temperature for up to 2 weeks.

Makes about 30 cookies

Chocolate Pound Cake

6 oz (185 g) unsweetened chocolate, chopped (1¼ cups)

1 lb (500 g) unsalted butter, at room temperature

1 cup (8 oz/250 g) sugar

6 extra-large eggs, at room temperature

2 teaspoons vanilla extract (essence)

2 cups (8 oz/250 g) all-purpose (plain) flour, sifted before measuring

1 cup (8 fl oz/250 ml) heavy (double) cream, whipped

This is delicious by itself, or topped with a scoop of vanilla ice cream. You can also use it to make the cassata alla siciliana on page 96.

*P*osition a rack in the middle of an oven and preheat the oven to 350°F (180°C). Butter and flour a 9-inch (23-cm) springform or tube pan.

Place the chocolate in a small heatproof bowl or the top pan of a double boiler. Set over a pan of gently simmering water but not touching the water. Stir until melted and smooth. Remove from the heat and let cool.

Place the butter and sugar in a large bowl. Using an electric mixer set on high speed, beat until light and fluffy, about 5 minutes. Add the eggs, one at a time, mixing well after each addition. Mix in the vanilla extract. Reduce the speed to low and beat in the cooled chocolate. Using a rubber spatula, fold in the sifted flour, mixing only until no traces of flour are visible. Pour and scrape the batter into the prepared pan and smooth the top.

Bake until the edges just start to pull away from the sides of the pan, about 1 hour. Transfer to a wire rack and let cool completely in the pan. To remove from the springform pan, release and remove the sides, invert the rack on the cake, invert the cake and rack together and lift off the pan bottom. If you are using a tube pan, invert the rack on the cake, then invert the cake and rack together and lift off the pan. Top each serving with a dab of the whipped cream.

Makes one 9-inch (23-cm) cake; serves 12

Heidi's Chocolate Butter Crisps

1 tablespoon unsweetened cocoa (not Dutch-process type)

½ teaspoon ground cinnamon

1½ cups (6 oz/180 g) all-purpose (plain) flour, sifted before measuring

1 cup (8 oz/250 g) unsalted butter, at room temperature

5 tablespoons (3 oz/90 g) granulated sugar

1½ teaspoons vanilla extract (essence)

¾ cup (3 oz/90 g) finely chopped nuts (see note)

⅔ cup (3⅓ oz/100 g) semisweet or bittersweet chocolate chips

½ cup (3 oz/90 g) confectioners' (icing) sugar

If you ever become tired of old-fashioned chocolate chip cookies, try these buttery alternatives. You may use finely chopped walnuts, toasted hazelnuts (filberts) or pecans. If you chop the nuts in a food processor, add 2–5 tablespoons of the sugar to the processor with the nuts to keep them from turning into nut butter.

Position a rack in the middle of an oven and preheat the oven to 350°F (180°C). Have ready 2 ungreased baking sheets.

Sift together the cocoa, cinnamon and sifted flour into a small bowl. Set aside. Place the butter and granulated sugar in a bowl. Using a whisk or an electric mixer set on high speed, beat until light and fluffy, 5–7 minutes with a whisk or 3–5 minutes with a mixer. Stir in the vanilla, nuts and chocolate chips. Gradually stir in the flour mixture, combining thoroughly.

Using a teaspoon scoop up rounded spoonfuls of the dough in the shape of large marbles and arrange 1 inch (2.5 cm) apart on the baking sheets.

Bake until golden brown, about 12 minutes. Let cool for 1 or 2 minutes, then dust with the confectioners' sugar.

Makes about 4½ dozen cookies

Sweet Chocolate Pie

chocolate crumb crust (recipe on
  page 15)
⅓ cup (3 fl oz/80 ml) heavy (double)
  cream
3 tablespoons instant-coffee granules
4 oz (125 g) semisweet chocolate,
  chopped (scant 1 cup)
1 lb (500 g) cream cheese, softened
2 extra-large eggs
¾ cup (6 oz/180 g) sugar
1 teaspoon vanilla extract (essence)
1½ cups (12 fl oz/375 ml) chocolate
  whipped cream (recipe on page 13)
strawberries, raspberries or chocolate
  coffee beans for topping

*This new take on chocolate cheesecake yields a divine
combination of chocolate textures and tastes, between the dark
chocolate cookie crumb crust, the smooth baked cream cheese
filling and the ethereally light chocolate cream topping. A perfect
birthday celebration dessert.*

*P*repare the chocolate crumb crust in a 10-inch (25-cm) pie
plate. Prebake as directed, then cool.

Preheat an oven to 325°F (165°C).

Gently warm the cream in a small saucepan over medium
heat until bubbles form at the edges. Add the coffee and stir
to dissolve. Set aside.

Place the chocolate in a small heatproof bowl or the top
pan of a double boiler. Set over a pan of gently simmering
water but not touching the water. Stir until melted and
smooth. Let cool slightly.

Place the cream cheese, eggs, sugar and vanilla in the bowl
of a food processor or in a mixing bowl. Process for 10
seconds or beat with an electric mixer set on low speed until
very smooth. Stir in the coffee mixture, then the cooled
chocolate. Pour and scrape into the cooled pie shell,
smoothing the top.

Bake until the top is dry to the touch and slightly firm,
35–45 minutes. Transfer to a wire rack to cool completely.
Top with the chocolate whipped cream and garnish with
berries or chocolate coffee beans.

Makes one 10-inch (25-cm) pie; serves 8

Chocolate Raspberry Bars

3 oz (90 g) unsweetened chocolate,
    chopped (scant ⅔ cup)
½ cup (4 oz/125 g) unsalted butter
1 cup (4 oz/125 g) all-purpose (plain)
    flour, sifted before measuring
½ teaspoon baking powder
2 extra-large eggs, at room
    temperature
1 cup (8 oz/250 g) sugar
1 teaspoon vanilla extract (essence)
½ cup (5 oz/155 g) raspberry
    preserves
sliced almonds for topping

All the flavors of the most sophisticated European dessert—raspberry, chocolate and almonds—come together in this easy-to-prepare American classic.

Position a rack in the middle of an oven and preheat the oven to 350°F (180°C). Grease a 9-inch (23-cm) square baking pan with butter or vegetable shortening.

Place the chocolate and butter in a small heatproof bowl or the top pan of a double boiler. Set over a pan of gently simmering water but not touching the water. Stir until melted and smooth. Let cool slightly.

Sift together the sifted flour and baking powder. Set aside.

Place the eggs and sugar in a bowl. Using a whisk or an electric mixer set on high speed, beat until thick and light colored, 5–8 minutes with a whisk or 3–5 minutes with a mixer. Stir in the cooled chocolate mixture and the vanilla. Stir in the flour mixture just until combined.

Pour and scrape the batter into the prepared pan, smoothing the top with a rubber spatula. Bake for 25–30 minutes.

Transfer to a wire rack to cool for 15 minutes, then spread the raspberry preserves on top. Sprinkle with almonds. Cut into bars while still warm, then let cool completely before removing from the pan.

Makes 12 bars

Cocoa Meringue Kisses

4 extra-large egg whites, at room
  temperature

pinch of cream of tartar

1 cup (8 oz/250 g) sugar

3 tablespoons unsweetened cocoa (not
  Dutch-process type), sifted after
  measuring

1 cup (5 oz/155 g) semisweet chocolate
  chips or coarsely chopped
  bittersweet chocolate

*The two secrets of success to these melt-in-your-mouth morsels
are to make them in dry weather and to use cocoa powder that is
not the Dutch-process type. You can make these with chocolate
chips or chunks of chocolate.*

*P*osition a rack in the upper third (not the highest point)
of an oven and preheat the oven to 275°F (135°C). Line a
heavy-duty baking sheet with parchment paper or
aluminum foil, shiny side down.

Place the egg whites and cream of tartar in a bowl. Using
an electric mixer set on medium speed, beat until foamy.
Increase the speed to high and continue beating while
gradually adding the sugar. Beat until stiff and quite glossy
but not dry. Reduce the speed to low and mix in the sifted
cocoa just until it is incorporated. Using a rubber spatula,
fold in the chocolate.

Using a tablespoon scoop up rather high mounds about
2 inches (5 cm) in diameter and place them 1 inch (2.5 cm)
apart on the prepared sheet.

Bake for 1 hour. The kisses should not color; if they begin
to brown, reduce the oven temperature to 250°F (120°C).
Turn off the oven but leave the kisses in the oven with the
door closed for 1 hour longer.

Lift the kisses off the parchment or foil and let cool
completely. Store in a covered container at room
temperature for up to 1 month.

Makes 24 kisses

Chocolate Pecan Pie

For the pie crust:

1½ cups (7½ oz/235 g) all-purpose (plain) flour

½ teaspoon salt

½ cup (4 oz/125 g) vegetable shortening

3–4 tablespoons water

1½ cups (6 oz/185 g) pecans, coarsely chopped

6 oz (180 g) semisweet chocolate chips (scant 1¼ cups)

¼ cup (2 oz/60 g) unsalted butter, softened

½ cup (4 fl oz/125 ml) light corn syrup

½ cup (3 oz/90 g) firmly packed dark brown sugar

2 extra-large eggs

2 teaspoons vanilla extract (essence)

Cut out leaves or other shapes from the pastry scraps and use them to top the pie. If you're short on time, buy refrigerated (not frozen) pie crust dough. Or make the dough recipe in a food processor: Place the flour, salt and shortening in the processor bowl fitted with the metal blade and pulse until crumbly. Add water gradually and pulse just to form a rough mass.

Position a rack in the middle of an oven and preheat the oven to 350°F (180°C). To make the pie crust, in a bowl stir together the flour and salt. Add the shortening and, using your fingertips, a pastry blender or two knives, blend until the mixture resembles coarse crumbs. Sprinkle on the water, 1 tablespoon at a time, stirring gently after each addition. Add water only until the dough forms a rough mass. Pat into a disk and, on a floured surface, roll out ⅛ inch (3 mm) thick and 12 inches (30 cm) in diameter. Transfer to a 9-inch (23-cm) pie pan and trim and flute the edges. Prick the bottom of the pie crust in several places with a fork.

Place in the oven and bake for 10 minutes. If the crust puffs up during baking, prick with a fork. Remove from the oven. Reduce the temperature to 325°F (165°C).

Sprinkle the pecans and chocolate chips evenly over the pie crust. In a small bowl beat together the butter, corn syrup, brown sugar, eggs and vanilla until smooth. Pour slowly and evenly over the nuts and chips so as not to disturb them. Continue to bake until set and slightly firm, about 50 minutes. Transfer to a wire rack to cool completely. Serve at room temperature.

Makes one 9-inch (23-cm) pie; serves 8–10

Chocolate Mint Squares

2 oz (60 g) unsweetened chocolate, chopped (rounded ⅓ cup)

2 oz (60 g) semisweet chocolate, chopped (rounded ⅓ cup)

¾ cup (6 oz/180 g) unsalted butter, at room temperature

¾ cup (3 oz/90 g) all-purpose (plain) flour, sifted before measuring

½ teaspoon baking soda (bicarbonate of soda)

½ cup (4 oz/125 g) granulated sugar

½ cup (3 oz/90 g) firmly packed light brown sugar

2 extra-large eggs

1 teaspoon peppermint extract (essence)

1⅓ cups (6 oz/180 g) mint chocolate chips

FOR THE FROSTING:

1 cup (4 oz/125 g) confectioners' (icing) sugar, sifted after measuring

3–4 tablespoons (2 fl oz/60 ml) milk

1½ teaspoons peppermint extract (essence)

several drops green food coloring, optional

Richer than brownies, with a hint of mint. You can serve them with or without the frosting. For a special presentation, drizzle some melted semisweet or bittersweet chocolate over the top.

*P*osition a rack in the middle of an oven and preheat the oven to 350°F (180°C). Grease an 8-inch (20-cm) square baking pan with butter or vegetable shortening.

Place the unsweetened and semisweet chocolates and the butter in a small heatproof bowl or the top pan of a double boiler. Set over a pan of gently simmering water but not touching the water. Stir until melted and smooth. Let cool briefly.

Sift together the sifted flour and baking soda into a bowl. Set aside. In another bowl combine the white and brown sugars and the eggs. Using a whisk or an electric mixer set on medium speed, beat until thick and light in consistency, 7–8 minutes with a whisk or 2–3 minutes with a mixer. Stir in the mint extract and then the cooled chocolate mixture. Add the flour mixture and then the mint chocolate chips, mixing just until incorporated (if using a mixer, reduce the speed to low for this step). Pour into the prepared pan. Bake until the top looks dry, about 30 minutes.

Meanwhile, prepare the frosting: Place the sifted confectioners' sugar in a bowl and add enough of the milk to form a paste with the consistency of heavy (double) cream. Stir in the mint extract and the food coloring, if using. Cover until ready to use.

Transfer the cake to a wire rack and let cool for 10 minutes, then pour on the frosting and spread evenly with a metal spatula. Let cool completely, then cut into 2-inch (5-cm) squares. Store in a covered container at room temperature for up to 1 week.

Makes 16 squares

Pecan Brownies

½ cup (2 oz/60 g) all-purpose (plain) flour, sifted before measuring
½ teaspoon baking powder
¾ cup (6 oz/185 g) granulated sugar
½ cup (3 oz/90 g) firmly packed dark brown sugar
½ cup (4 oz/125 g) unsalted butter, at room temperature
2 oz (60 g) unsweetened chocolate, chopped (rounded ⅓ cup)
1 tablespoon light corn syrup
2 large eggs
1 teaspoon vanilla extract (essence)
1½ cups (6 oz/185 g) pecan halves, broken into pieces

This recipe calls for unsweetened chocolate, which gives the brownies a maximum chocolate impact. Substitute walnuts for the pecans if you wish.

*P*osition a rack in the middle of an oven and preheat the oven to 350°F (180°C). Butter and flour an 8-inch (20-cm) square baking pan.

Sift together the sifted flour and baking powder into a bowl. Set aside.

In a small saucepan set over low heat, combine the granulated and dark brown sugars, butter, chocolate and corn syrup. Stir continuously until the mixture is smooth. Remove from the heat, pour into a large bowl and let cool until just warm to the touch.

Add the eggs and vanilla to the chocolate mixture, and then add the flour mixture and pecans, stirring only until just combined. Pour and scrape the batter into the prepared pan, smoothing the top.

Bake until the top looks dry, about 35 minutes; do not overbake. Transfer to a wire rack and let cool completely, then cut into squares. Store in a covered container at room temperature for up to 1 week.

Makes about 16 brownies

Chocolate Pecan Quick Bread

5 eggs, separated and at room
  temperature
¾ cup (6 oz/185 g) sugar
¼ cup (2 oz/60 g) unsalted butter,
  melted and cooled slightly
1 teaspoon vanilla extract (essence)
1 cup (4 oz/125 g) all-purpose (plain)
  flour, sifted before measuring
¼ teaspoon ground cinnamon
3 oz (90 g) unsweetened chocolate,
  finely chopped (scant ⅔ cup)
1 cup (4 oz/125 g) ground pecans,
  almonds or toasted hazelnuts
  (filberts)
3 cups (24 fl oz/750 ml) chocolate
  whipped cream (recipe on page 13)

*This simple-looking loaf doesn't rise very high, but it has an
elegant and sophisticated flavor and a lovely, moist texture.*

*P*osition a rack in the middle of an oven and preheat the
oven to 375°F (190°C). Butter and flour an 8½-by-4½-by-
2½-inch (21-by-11-by-6-cm) loaf pan.

   Place the egg whites and about half of the sugar in a bowl.
Using an electric mixer set on high speed, beat until stiff and
shiny, but not dry. Set aside.

   In a separate bowl combine the egg yolks and the
remaining sugar and beat on high speed until thick and light
colored, 3–5 minutes. Beat in the melted butter and vanilla.

   Sift together the sifted flour and cinnamon into a large
bowl. Stir into the yolk mixture, mixing just until
completely incorporated. Stir in half the beaten egg whites,
then gently fold in the remaining egg whites. Fold in the
chocolate and nuts. Pour and scrape the batter into the
prepared pan. Smooth the top with a rubber spatula,
mounding it slightly higher along the center.

   Bake until a toothpick inserted in the center comes out
clean and dry, 45–50 minutes. Cool in the pan for 15
minutes, then invert onto a rack to cool completely. Serve
with the chocolate whipped cream.

Makes 1 loaf cake; serves 8

Chocolate Angel Pie

4 extra-large egg whites, at room
   temperature

¼ teaspoon cream of tartar

⅔ cup (5 oz/155 g) sugar

2 tablespoons unsweetened cocoa (not
   Dutch-process type)

1 cup (8 fl oz/250 ml) heavy (double)
   cream, whipped with 2 tablespoons
   sugar

miniature chocolate chips for topping

*Top with fresh berries or chocolate shavings in place of the chips,
if you like. For a pie with a softer texture, refrigerate for 1 hour
after topping with the whipped cream.*

*P*osition a rack in the middle of an oven and preheat the
oven to 300°F (150°C). Generously butter a 10-inch (25-
cm) pie plate with 2-inch (5-cm) sides. Dust with flour and
tap out any excess.

   Place the egg whites, cream of tartar and sugar in a bowl.
Using an electric mixer set on high speed, beat until stiff and
glossy but not dry. Reduce the speed to low and beat in the
cocoa, mixing only until incorporated.

   Pour and scrape the batter into the prepared pie plate. Use
a rubber spatula to smooth the top, building the rim slightly
higher than the center.

   Bake until the egg whites are light brown and no longer
sticky, about 1 hour. Transfer to a wire rack to cool
completely. The center will sink as it cools.

   Just before serving, fill the center with the whipped cream.
Sprinkle with miniature chocolate chips.

Makes one 10-inch (25-cm) pie; serves 8

Chocolate Layer Cake

1¾ cups (6 oz/185 g) cake (soft-wheat)
flour, sifted before measuring

1 teaspoon baking soda (bicarbonate
of soda)

1½ teaspoons baking powder

½ cup (4 fl oz/125 ml) milk

3 oz (90 g) unsweetened chocolate,
coarsely chopped (scant ⅔ cup)

1 cup (8 fl oz/250 ml) sour cream

1 cup (8 oz/250 g) granulated sugar

⅔ cup (5 oz/155 g) firmly packed
dark brown sugar

¾ cup (6 oz/185 g) unsalted butter, at
room temperature

2 teaspoons vanilla extract (essence)

3 extra-large eggs

chocolate whipped cream (*recipe on
page 13*)

*This splendid confection makes the perfect birthday celebration cake.
You can also use ½ recipe chocolate whipped cream between the layers
and cover the top with lukewarm chocolate ganache (recipe on page 12).*

*P*osition a rack in the middle of an oven and preheat the oven to
350°F (180°C). Butter two 9-inch (23-cm) layer cake pans. Line
the bottoms with parchment paper or waxed paper cut to fit
precisely. Butter the paper and dust with flour; tap out any excess.

Sift together the sifted flour, baking soda and baking powder
into a bowl. Set aside.

In a small saucepan set over medium heat, gently warm the
milk until small bubbles appear at the edges. Remove from the
heat and whisk in the chocolate until it melts and the mixture is
smooth. Let cool completely. Stir in the sour cream.

Combine the granulated and brown sugars and the butter in a
bowl. Using an electric mixer set on high speed, beat until fluffy,
3–5 minutes. Reduce to medium speed and beat in the vanilla.
Add the eggs, one at a time, mixing well after each addition. On
low speed beat in the flour mixture alternately with the chocolate
mixture; mix only until the ingredients are incorporated.

Pour the batter into the prepared pans and smooth the tops.
Bake until the edges start to pull away from the pan sides and a
toothpick inserted in the center comes out clean, 30–40 minutes.
Transfer to wire racks. Let cool in the pans for 15 minutes, then
unmold onto racks to cool completely. Peel off the paper.

Place 1 cake layer on a serving plate. Spread with half of the
chocolate whipped cream. Top with the remaining cake layer and
spread with the remaining whipped cream.

Makes one 9-inch (23-cm) layer cake; serves 8–10

Cassata alla Siciliana

This dessert is a specialty of a wonderful Italian restaurant in Provincetown, Massachusetts, called Ciro and Sal's. They make it with white pound cake, but I prefer chocolate. Choose whatever flavor cake you please, store-bought or homemade. If you use the recipe on page 64, bake it in a standard loaf pan and use the extra batter for cupcakes.

To make the frosting, place the chocolate, butter and espresso in a small heatproof bowl or the top pan of a double boiler. Set over a pan of gently simmering water but not touching the water. Stir until melted, smooth and thoroughly combined. Remove the bowl from the heat and refrigerate, stirring every 15 minutes, until firm, about 1 hour. (To firm up the frosting more quickly, nest the bowl in a bowl of ice and stir it every 5 minutes. It will take 15–20 minutes to become firm.)

In a bowl stir together the ricotta, sugar and orange zest. Using a plastic or metal grater, grate the chunk of chocolate into the bowl and fold it in using a rubber spatula.

Using a serrated knife, cut the pound cake twice horizontally to form 3 equal layers. Place one layer on a flat plate and sprinkle 2 tablespoons of the liqueur over it. Spread half of the ricotta mixture on top. Top with the second layer, sprinkle with the remaining 2 tablespoons liqueur and spread with the remaining ricotta mixture. Top with the third layer. Using a narrow metal spatula, frost the top and sides with the cooled chocolate mixture. Refrigerate until serving, but no longer than 8 hours.

Serves 8

For the frosting:

4 oz (125 g) semisweet chocolate, chopped (scant 1 cup)

6 oz (185 g) unsalted butter, at room temperature

½ cup (4 fl oz/125 ml) brewed espresso, or 1 tablespoon instant espresso powder or granules dissolved in ½ cup (4 fl oz/125 ml) boiling water

For the cake:

2 cups (1 lb/500 g) whole-milk ricotta cheese

¼ cup (1 oz/30 g) confectioners' (icing) sugar

finely grated zest of 1 orange

2–3 oz (60–90 g) sweet, semisweet, bittersweet or milk chocolate, in one thick chunk

1 chocolate pound cake, store-bought or homemade (*recipe on page 64*)

4 tablespoons (2 fl oz/60 ml) orange-flavored liqueur

Chocolate Chip Scones

2 cups (8 oz/250 g) all-purpose (plain) flour, sifted before measuring, plus flour for working

1 tablespoon baking powder

½ teaspoon salt

¼ cup (2 oz/60 g) sugar, plus 2–3 tablespoons

¾ cup (3¾ oz/115 g) semisweet chocolate chips or about 4 oz (125 g) semisweet chocolate, roughly broken into ½-inch (12-mm) pieces

1¼ cups (10 fl oz/310 ml) heavy (double) cream

3 tablespoons unsalted butter, melted

These are an unusual breakfast treat, or spread them with butter or jam for a special teatime pick-me-up. You may use chocolate chips or break a bar of chocolate into pieces. They do not keep well, so eat them all the day they are baked.

*P*osition a rack in the middle of an oven and preheat the oven to 425°F (220°C). Select a heavy-duty baking sheet but do not grease it.

Sift together the sifted flour, baking powder, salt and the ¼ cup (2 oz/60 g) sugar into a bowl. Toss together with a fork to mix thoroughly. Mix in the chocolate chips or pieces. Pour in the cream and mix with the fork until the mixture holds together. The dough will be fairly sticky.

Transfer the dough to a lightly floured work surface and sprinkle lightly with flour. Knead the dough 10 times, pushing it away from you with the heel of your hand, folding it back over itself and giving it a quarter-turn each time. Pat into a 9-inch (23-cm) disk. Brush with the melted butter and then sprinkle with the 2–3 tablespoons sugar. Cut the dough into 12 pie-shaped wedges and transfer each to the baking sheet, leaving about a 1-inch (2.5-cm) space between the wedges.

Bake until the tops are golden brown, 15–17 minutes. Serve warm or at room temperature.

Makes 12 scones

Nuts

Rich and mellow in flavor, crisp and crunchy in texture, a wide variety of nuts complements recipes featuring chocolate. For the best selection, look in a specialty-food shop, health-food store or the food market baking section. Some of the most popular options include:

Almonds

Mellow, sweet-flavored nuts (below) that are an important crop in California and are popular throughout the world.

Brazil Nuts

Large, slightly astringent nutmeats native to Brazil, where they grow in hard, brown triangular shells and have white meats and thin brown skins.

Cashews

Kidney-shaped, crisp nuts with a slightly sweet and buttery flavor. Native to tropical America but grown throughout the world, primarily India.

Hazelnuts

Small, usually spherical nuts (below) with a slightly sweet flavor. Grown in Italy, Spain and the United States. Also known as filberts.

Macadamias

Spherical nuts (below), about twice the diameter of hazelnuts, with a very rich, buttery flavor and crisp texture. Native to Australia, they are now grown primarily in Hawaii.

Peanuts

Not true nuts, these are actually legumes produced on a low-branching plant. When roasted, they have a rich, full flavor and satisfying crispness that make them the world's most popular nut. The Virginia variety is longer and more oval than the smaller, rounder, red-skinned Spanish peanut. Native to South America, peanuts are an important crop in Africa and the United States.

Pecans

Brown-skinned, crinkly textured nuts (below) with a distinctive sweet, rich flavor and crisp, slightly crumbly texture. Native to the southern United States.

Pistachios

Slightly sweet, full-flavored nuts with distinctively green, crunchy meat. Native to Asia Minor, they are grown primarily in the Middle East and California.

Walnuts

Rich, crisp-textured nuts with distinctively crinkled surfaces. English walnuts, the most familiar variety, are grown worldwide, although the largest crops are in California. American black walnuts, sold primarily as shelled pieces, have a stronger flavor that lends extra distinction to desserts and candies.

To Blanch Nuts

Some nuts, such as almonds, require blanching to loosen their papery skin. To blanch nuts, put them in a pan of boiling water for about 2 minutes; then drain and, when they are cool enough to handle, squeeze each nut between your fingers to slip it from its skin.

To Toast Nuts

Toasting brings out the full flavor and aroma of nuts. To toast any kind of nut, preheat an oven to 325°F (165°C). Spread the nuts in a single layer on a baking sheet and toast in the oven until they just begin to change color, 5–10 minutes. Remove from the oven and let cool to room temperature.

Toasting also loosens the skins of nuts such as hazelnuts and walnuts, which may be removed by wrapping the still-warm nuts in a cotton towel and rubbing against them with the palms of your hands.

To Chop Nuts

To chop nuts, spread them in a single layer on a nonslip cutting surface. Using a chef's knife, carefully chop the nuts with a gentle rocking motion.

Alternatively, put a handful or two of nuts in a food processor fitted with the metal blade and use a few rapid on-off pulses to chop the nuts to desired consistency; repeat with the remaining nuts in batches. Be careful not to process the nuts too long or their oils will be released and the nuts will turn into a paste.

To Grind Nuts

A nut mill, which attaches to a countertop with a clamp, is the best tool for grinding nuts evenly. Place the shelled nuts in the top compartment, called a hopper, and turn the hand crank. Some mills come with both small and medium-sized cutting teeth.

Alternatively, grind the nuts using a mortar and pestle or a food processor.

MARGARINE
Solid form of vegetable fat processed to resemble the taste, texture and appearance of **butter.** Although its flavor cannot compare to butter's full richness, margarine may be used as a substitute by those who wish to limit animal fats in their diet.

MILK
Unless otherwise specified, use fresh whole homogenized milk for the recipes in this book. Canned condensed or evaporated milk is whole milk from which approximately 60 percent of the water has been removed, resulting in an intensified flavor and consistency that enriches some dessert recipes. Sweetened condensed milk includes sugar.

PEARS
The subtle sweetness and texture of pears combines surprisingly well with chocolate's richness. Anjou pears, available from autumn through mid-spring, are rich in flavor, with a hint of spice and a smooth texture; among the largest and plumpest of pears, they have short necks and thin, yellow-green skins. Bartlett pears, also called Williams' pears, are medium-sized and shaped roughly like bells, with creamy yellow skins sometimes tinged in red; fine-textured, juicy and mild-tasting, they are equally good for cooking or eating and are available from summer to early autumn. Comice pears, available from autumn through early winter, are sweet and juicy; large, round and short-necked, they have green-ish yellow skins tinged with red.

PEPPERMINT EXTRACT
Flavoring derived by dissolving the essential oil of fresh peppermint leaves in an alcohol base. Use only products labeled "pure" or "natural" peppermint extract (essence).

SIFTING
Passing fine-textured ingredients such as flour or sugar through a fine-mesh screen (usually a special sifting tool) to loosen its particles, remove lumps and lighten its texture.

SUGAR, BROWN
Granulated sugar combined with molasses in varying quantities to yield light or dark varieties of moist, fine-textured, rich-tasting sugar.

SUGAR, CONFECTIONERS'
A finely pulverized form of sugar, also known as powdered or icing sugar, which dissolves quickly. To prevent it from absorbing moisture in the air and caking, manufacturers often mix a little **cornstarch** into it.

SUGAR, GRANULATED
The standard, widely used form of pure white sugar.

SUGAR, SUPERFINE
Granulated sugar ground to form extra-fine granules that dissolve quickly in liquids and are ideal for some baking recipes. In Britain use castor sugar.

TRUFFLES
Chocolate candies made from **ganache** mixed with extracts, liqueurs or other flavorings and formed into irregular-shaped round balls that—coated as they sometimes are with cocoa powder—fancifully resemble the form of subterranean, earthy fungus for which they are named.

VANILLA EXTRACT
Flavoring derived by dissolving the essential oil of the vanilla bean in an alcohol base. Use only products labeled "pure" or "natural" vanilla extract (essence).

ZEST
Thin, brightly colored, outermost layer of a citrus fruit's peel, containing most of its aromatic essential oils—a lively source of flavor. Zest may be removed with a simple tool known as a zester, drawn across the fruit's skin to remove the zest in thin strips; with a fine hand-held grater; or in wide strips with a vegetable peeler or a paring knife held almost parallel to the fruit's skin. Zest removed with the latter two tools may then be thinly sliced or chopped on a cutting board.

PANS, CAKE
To facilitate neat unmolding of cakes, the pans in which they are baked usually require simple greasing and lining with parchment or waxed paper before they are filled with batter:

1. Peel back the wrapper on a softened stick of butter and rub the butter gently but firmly over the inside bottom and sides of the pan to coat evenly.

2. Place the pan on a large sheet of parchment or waxed paper and, using a pencil, trace a line around the bottom of the pan. Using scissors, cut out the circle just inside the pencil line drawn on the paper.

3. Slip the paper circle into the pan. Butter the paper, then dust with flour, tapping out the excess.

4. After the cake is baked and has cooled for a few minutes on a rack, loosen it by running a blunt knife around the sides.

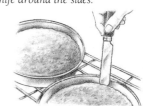

5. To unmold the cake, use pot holders, oven mitts or kitchen towels to clasp another wire rack firmly on top of the pan. Quickly invert the rack and pan together; then lift off the pan and peel the paper from the cake.

MARGARINE
Solid form of vegetable fat processed to resemble the taste, texture and appearance of **butter.** Although its flavor cannot compare to butter's full richness, margarine may be used as a substitute by those who wish to limit animal fats in their diet.

MILK
Unless otherwise specified, use fresh whole homogenized milk for the recipes in this book. Canned condensed or evaporated milk is whole milk from which approximately 60 percent of the water has been removed, resulting in an intensified flavor and consistency that enriches some dessert recipes. Sweetened condensed milk includes sugar.

PEARS
The subtle sweetness and texture of pears combines surprisingly well with chocolate's richness. Anjou pears, available from autumn through mid-spring, are rich in flavor, with a hint of spice and a smooth texture; among the largest and plumpest of pears, they have short necks and thin, yellow-green skins. Bartlett pears, also called Williams' pears, are medium-sized and shaped roughly like bells, with creamy yellow skins sometimes tinged in red; fine-textured, juicy and mild-tasting, they are equally good for cooking or eating and are available from summer to early autumn. Comice pears, available from autumn through early winter, are sweet and juicy; large, round and short-necked, they have green-ish yellow skins tinged with red.

PEPPERMINT EXTRACT
Flavoring derived by dissolving the essential oil of fresh peppermint leaves in an alcohol base. Use only products labeled "pure" or "natural" peppermint extract (essence).

SIFTING
Passing fine-textured ingredients such as flour or sugar through a fine-mesh screen (usually a special sifting tool) to loosen its particles, remove lumps and lighten its texture.

SUGAR, BROWN
Granulated sugar combined with molasses in varying quantities to yield light or dark varieties of moist, fine-textured, rich-tasting sugar.

SUGAR, CONFECTIONERS'
A finely pulverized form of sugar, also known as powdered or icing sugar, which dissolves quickly. To prevent it from absorbing moisture in the air and caking, manufacturers often mix a little **cornstarch** into it.

SUGAR, GRANULATED
The standard, widely used form of pure white sugar.

SUGAR, SUPERFINE
Granulated sugar ground to form extra-fine granules that dissolve quickly in liquids and are ideal for some baking recipes. In Britain use castor sugar.

TRUFFLES
Chocolate candies made from **ganache** mixed with extracts, liqueurs or other flavorings and formed into irregular-shaped round balls that—coated as they sometimes are with cocoa powder—fancifully resemble the form of subterranean, earthy fungus for which they are named.

VANILLA EXTRACT
Flavoring derived by dissolving the essential oil of the vanilla bean in an alcohol base. Use only products labeled "pure" or "natural" vanilla extract (essence).

ZEST
Thin, brightly colored, outermost layer of a citrus fruit's peel, containing most of its aromatic essential oils—a lively source of flavor. Zest may be removed with a simple tool known as a zester, drawn across the fruit's skin to remove the zest in thin strips; with a fine hand-held grater; or in wide strips with a vegetable peeler or a paring knife held almost parallel to the fruit's skin. Zest removed with the latter two tools may then be thinly sliced or chopped on a cutting board.

PANS, CAKE
To facilitate neat unmolding of cakes, the pans in which they are baked usually require simple greasing and lining with parchment or waxed paper before they are filled with batter:

1. Peel back the wrapper on a softened stick of butter and rub the butter gently but firmly over the inside bottom and sides of the pan to coat evenly.

2. Place the pan on a large sheet of parchment or waxed paper and, using a pencil, trace a line around the bottom of the pan. Using scissors, cut out the circle just inside the pencil line drawn on the paper.

3. Slip the paper circle into the pan. Butter the paper, then dust with flour, tapping out the excess.

4. After the cake is baked and has cooled for a few minutes on a rack, loosen it by running a blunt knife around the sides.

5. To unmold the cake, use pot holders, oven mitts or kitchen towels to clasp another wire rack firmly on top of the pan. Quickly invert the rack and pan together; then lift off the pan and peel the paper from the cake.

Index

ACKNOWLEDGMENTS

The publishers would like to thank the following people and organizations for their generous assistance and support in producing this book:
Narsai David, Jody Adams, Sharon C. Lott, Tara Brown, James Obata, Ken DellaPenta, Stephen W. Griswold, the buyers for Gardener's Eden, and the buyers and store managers for Pottery Barn and Williams-Sonoma stores.

The following kindly lent props for the photography:
Biordi Art Imports, Fillamento, J. Goldsmith Antiques, Sue Fisher King, Karen Nicks, Lorraine and Judson Puckett, and Chuck Williams.